Copyright © 2021 by David J. Reimer Sr.
All photographs are were taken by the author.

All rights reserved, including the right to reproduce the book or portions thereof in any form or by any means, electronic or mechanical, including photocopying, recording, or by any information storage and retrieval system, without permission in writing from the publisher. All inquiries should be addressed to Crave Press, Leesport, PA.

Printed in the United States of America

FIRST EDITION

Paperback ISBN: 978-1-952352-10-2
Hardcover ISBN: 978-1-952352-11-9

Dedication

This book is dedicated to the people of Cuba who keep these old-school American beauties alive through their resourcefulness and ingenuity.

We tip our hats to you.

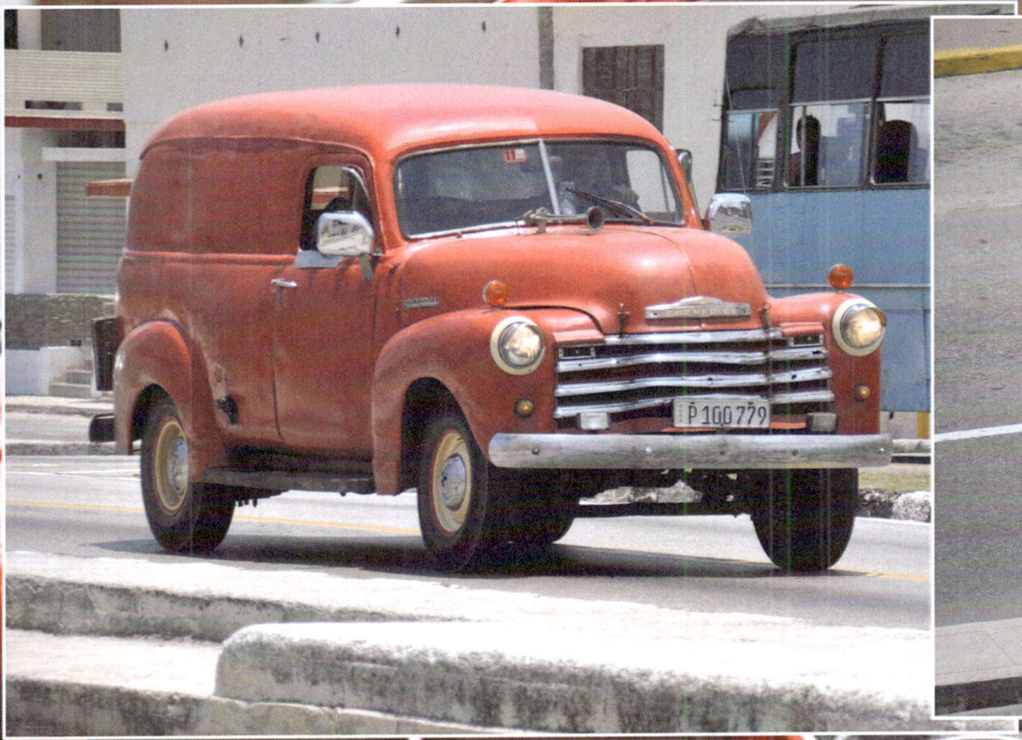
P 100779

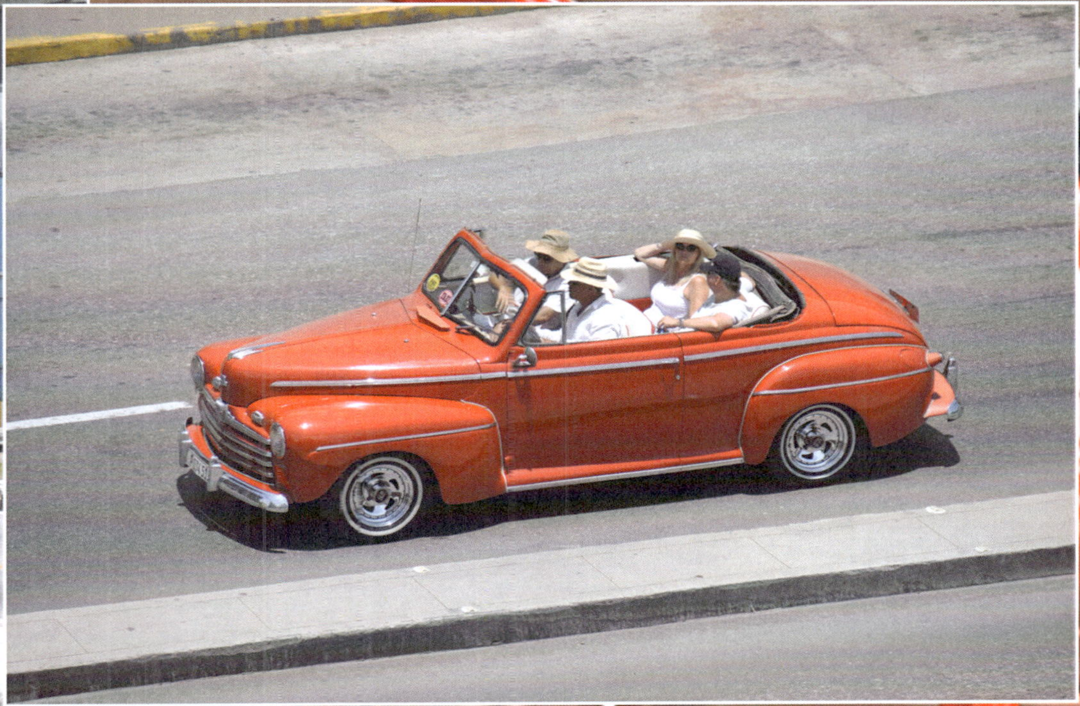

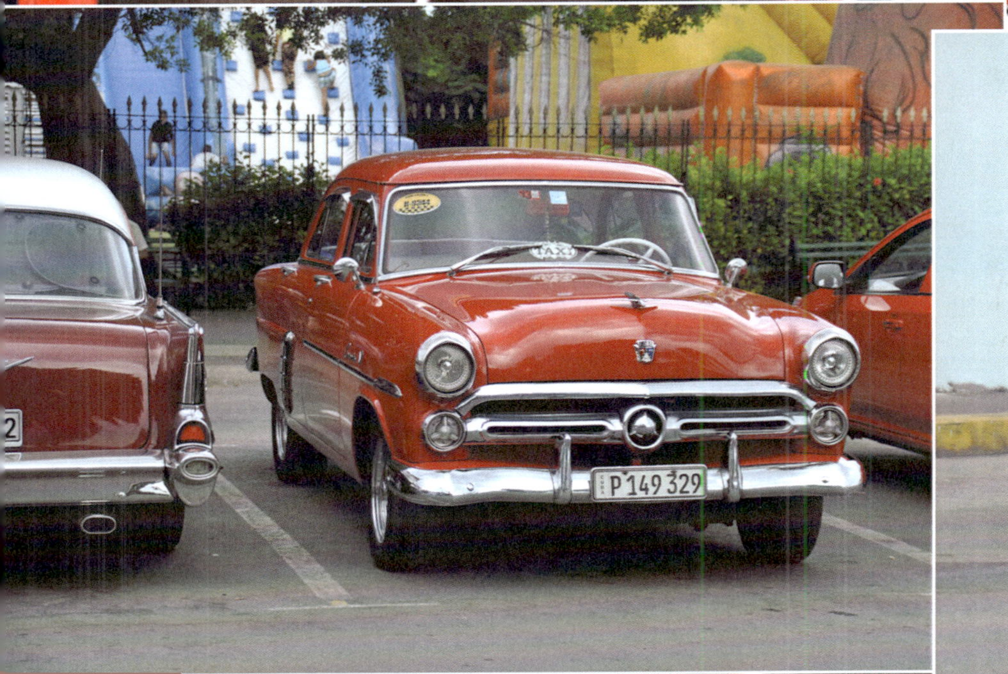
TAXI
P 149 329

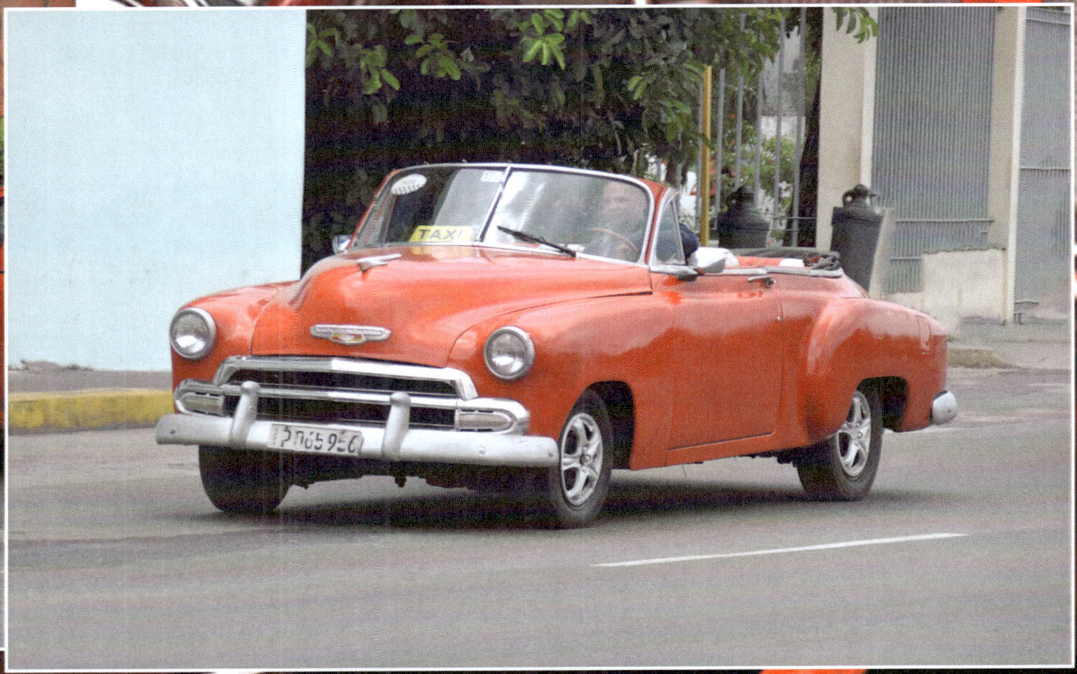
TAXI

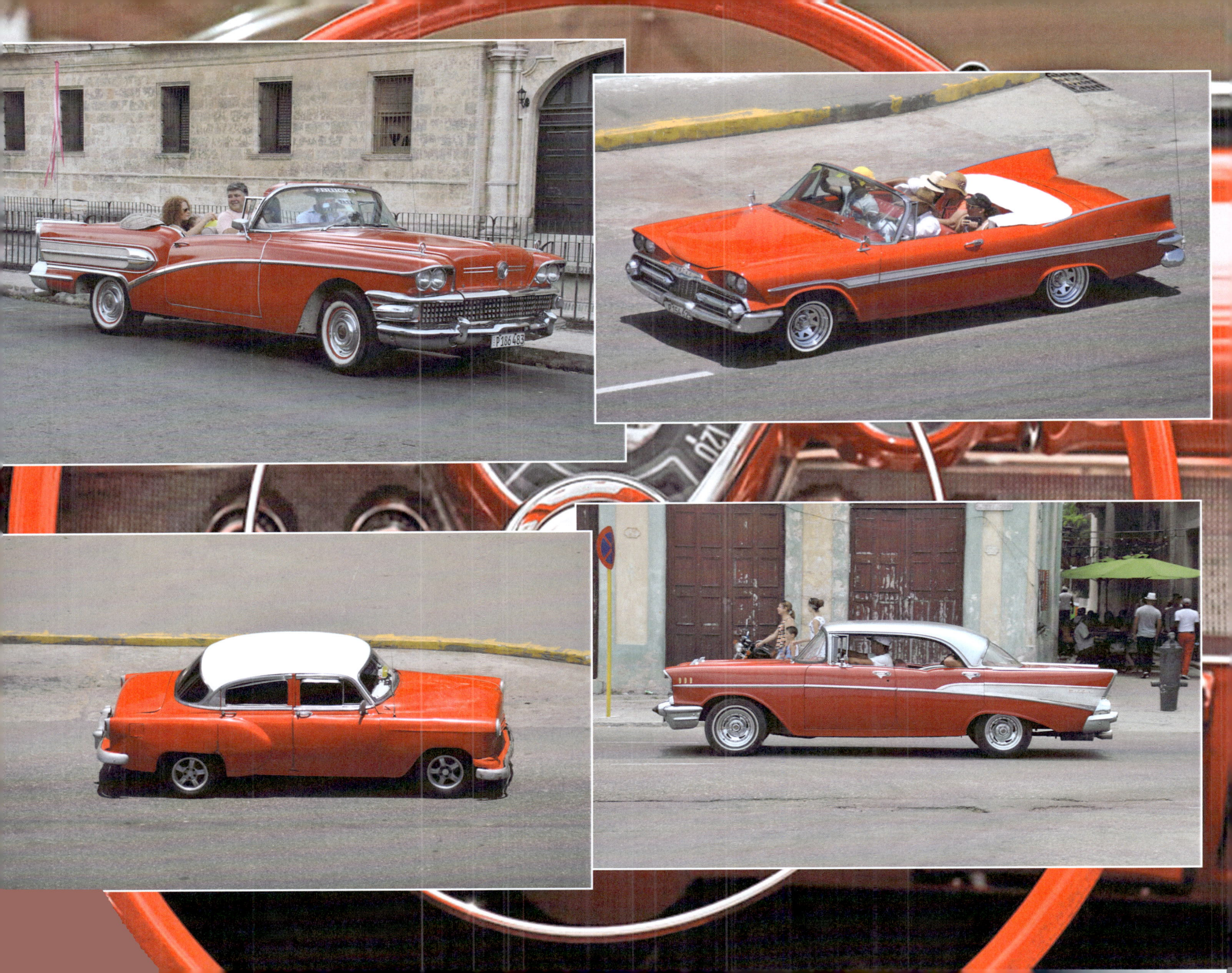